A+ books®

DINOSAUR FACT DIG

ANKYLOSAURUS
AND OTHER ARMOURED DINOSAURS
THE NEED-TO-KNOW FACTS

BY
KATHRYN CLAY

Consultant: Mathew J. Wedel, PhD
Associate Professor
Western University of Health Services

raintree

Raintree is an imprint of Capstone Global Library Limited, a company incorporated in England and Wales having its registered office at 264 Banbury Road, Oxford, OX2 7DY – Registered company number: 6695582

www.raintree.co.uk
myorders@raintree.co.uk
Text © Capstone Global Library Limited 2016
The moral rights of the proprietor have been asserted.

Edited by Michelle Hasselius
Designed by Kazuko Collins
Picture research by Wanda Winch
Production by Gene Bentdahl

ISBN 978 1 474 71937 7 (hardcover)
20 19 18 17 16
10 9 8 7 6 5 4 3 2 1

ISBN 978 1 474 71950 6 (paperback)
21 20 19 18 17
10 9 8 7 6 5 4 3 2 1

British Library Cataloguing in Publication Data
A full catalogue record for this book is available from the British Library.

ACKNOWLEDGEMENTS
All images by Jon Hughes except: MapArt (maps), Shuttershock: Elena Elisseeva, green gingko leaf, Jiang Hongyan, yellow gingko leaf, Taigi, paper background

Printed and bound in China.

CONTENTS

Whack! Meat-eating dinosaurs didn't stand a chance against Ankylosaurus and other armoured dinosaurs. Many of these giant armoured dinosaurs had clubbed tails, which they'd use to strike nearby predators.

These dinosaurs lived between 160 and 65 million years ago. Their bodies were covered in thick armour to protect them against enemies. Other armoured dinosaurs included the speedy Minmi and the tiny Scutellosaurus. Though different sizes, each found ways to guard against enemies.

ALETOPELTA

PRONOUNCED: ah-LET-o-PEL-ta

NAME MEANING: wandering shield

TIME PERIOD LIVED: Late Cretaceous Period, about 70 million years ago

LENGTH: 5 metres (16 feet)

WEIGHT: 2 metric tons (2.2 tons)

TYPE OF EATER: herbivore

PHYSICAL FEATURES: heavy shields and spikes around shoulders and neck, plates along tail

ALETOPELTA was named in 2001.

Eight **ALETOPELTA** teeth were found in California, USA.

Aletopelta lived in the mountains of western North America.

N
W E
S

■ where this dinosaur lived

After **ALETOPELTA** died, its body sank to the sea floor. It formed a tiny reef for ancient clams to live on.

ALETOPELTA had a club tail, like many dinosaurs in this group.

ANKYLOSAURUS

PRONOUNCED: ANG-kuh-lo-SAWR-us

NAME MEANING: fused lizard

TIME PERIOD LIVED: Late Cretaceous Period, about 65 million years ago

LENGTH: 9 metres (30 feet)

WEIGHT: 6 metric tons (6.5 tons)

TYPE OF EATER: herbivore

PHYSICAL FEATURES: body covered in armour except for stomach, bony club at the end of tail

ANKYLOSAURUS weighed about as much as a bull elephant today.

Ankylosaurus lived in western North America.

A whole **ANKYLOSAURUS** skeleton has never been found.

N
W — E
S

where this dinosaur lived

A model of **ANKYLOSAURUS** was displayed at the 1964 New York World's Fair, USA.

ANKYLOSAURUS even had armour protecting its eyelids.

A full-grown **ANKYLOSAURUS** could swing its club tail hard enough to break bones. The dinosaur's club was made from big tailbones that grew together.

EDMONTONIA

PRONOUNCED: ED-mun-TOH-nee-ah

NAME MEANING: named for the Edmonton Formation in Alberta, Canada, where its fossils were discovered

TIME PERIOD LIVED: Late Cretaceous Period, about 70 million years ago

LENGTH: 6 metres (20 feet)

WEIGHT: 3 metric tons (3.3 tons)

TYPE OF EATER: herbivore

PHYSICAL FEATURES: back covered with armour and large spikes, pointy beak

Three different **EDMONTONIA** species have been found.

EDMONTONIA travelled in herds.

Edmontonia lived in today's Montana, USA and Alberta, Canada.

where this dinosaur lived

Paleontologists know more about **EDMONTONIA** than other armoured dinosaurs because they have found complete skeletons.

EUOPLOCEPHALUS

PRONOUNCED: YOU-oh-plo-SEF-ah-lus

NAME MEANING: well-armoured head

TIME PERIOD LIVED: Late Cretaceous Period, about 70 million years ago

LENGTH: 6 metres (20 feet)

WEIGHT: 2 metric tons (2.2 tons)

TYPE OF EATER: herbivore

PHYSICAL FEATURES: ring of armour around its neck, club at end of tail

Several nearly complete skeletons of **EUOPLOCEPHALUS** have been found.

EUOPLOCEPHALUS had tiny teeth compared to its giant body. They were about as long as human teeth.

EUOPLOCEPHALUS was named Stereocephalus, but it had to be changed. An insect had the name first.

Euoplocephalus lived in western North America and Alberta, Canada.

N
W — E
S

where this dinosaur lived

GASTONIA

PRONOUNCED: gas-TOE-nee-ah

NAME MEANING: named after paleontologist Robert Gaston

TIME PERIOD LIVED: Early Cretaceous Period, about 125 million years ago

LENGTH: 5 metres (17 feet)

WEIGHT: 1.9 metric tons (2.1 tons)

TYPE OF EATER: herbivore

PHYSICAL FEATURES: covered with spikes and plates, row of small teeth

GASTONIA was one of the most common dinosaurs of its time.

GASTONIA'S belly was not protected by armour. A predator would have to flip Gastonia over to eat it.

Gastonia lived in western North America, near where Utah, USA is today.

N
W · E
S

where this
dinosaur lived

GASTONIA is related to
the dinosaur Polacanthus.

MINMI

PRONOUNCED: MIN-mee

NAME MEANING: named after Minmi's Crossing in Australia, where its fossils were discovered

TIME PERIOD LIVED: Early Cretaceous Period, about 115 million years ago

LENGTH: 3 metres (9 feet)

WEIGHT: 300 kilograms (600 pounds)

TYPE OF EATER: herbivore

PHYSICAL FEATURES: short spikes on hips and tail, hard plates on back and belly

MINMI was faster than other armoured dinosaurs.

Minmi lived in what is now Australia.

The name "**MINMI**" is one of the shortest dinosaur names.

N
W E
S

where this dinosaur lived

A nearly complete **MINMI** skeleton was found in Australia in 1987.

NODOSAURUS

PRONOUNCED: NOH-doe-SAWR-us

NAME MEANING: knobbed lizard

TIME PERIOD LIVED: Cretaceous Period, about 110 million years ago

LENGTH: 4 to 6.1 metres (13 to 20 feet)

WEIGHT: 2.5 metric tons (2.8 tons)

TYPE OF EATER: herbivore

PHYSICAL FEATURES: almost completely covered with heavy armour

No complete **NODOSAURUS** fossil has ever been found.

Nodosaurus lived in what is now Wyoming, USA.

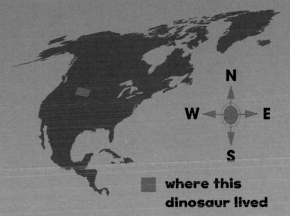

where this dinosaur lived

NODOSAURUS was one of the first armoured dinosaurs discovered. Its fossils were found in 1889.

NODOSAURUS was featured in the film *The Land Before Time 3*. The character's name was Nod.

PAWPAWSAURUS

PRONOUNCED: POOR-poor-SAWR-us

NAME MEANING: pawpaw lizard, fossils found in the Paw Paw Formation in Texas

TIME PERIOD LIVED: Early Cretaceous Period, about 100 years ago

LENGTH: 4.5 metres (15 feet)

WEIGHT: 0.9 metric ton (1 ton)

TYPE OF EATER: herbivore

PHYSICAL FEATURES: spikes on its shoulders and back, body covered with armour

PAWPAWSAURUS fossils were discovered in 1992.

Like many armoured dinosaurs, **PAWPAWSAURUS** had armoured eyelids.

Pawpawsaurus lived in North America, in what is now Texas, USA.

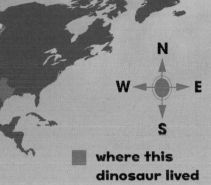

where this dinosaur lived

A complete **PAWPAWSAURUS** skeleton has never been found.

PAWPAWSAURUS had two rows of tiny teeth.

PAWPAWSAURUS needed armour to protect itself. It lived during the same time as the giant predator Acrocanthosaurus.

POLACANTHUS ✓

PRONOUNCED: POH-lah-KAN-thus

NAME MEANING: many spikes

TIME PERIOD LIVED: Early Cretaceous Period, about 130 million years ago

LENGTH: 5 metres (17 feet)

WEIGHT: 1.5 metric tons (1.7 tons)

TYPE OF EATER: herbivore

PHYSICAL FEATURES: hard plates on its tail and hips, sharp spikes on its shoulders

Paleontologists do not know if **POLACANTHUS** had a pointy beak or sharp teeth. This dinosaur's skull has never been found.

Polacanthus lived in parts of western Europe, in what is now southeast England.

N
W   E
S

☐ where this dinosaur lived

POLACANTHUS is related to Gastonia, another armoured dinosaur.

POLACANTHUS walked on four legs.

SCELIDOSAURUS

PRONOUNCED: skel-ih-doe-SAWR-us

NAME MEANING: limb lizard

TIME PERIOD LIVED: Early Jurassic Period, about 190 million years ago

LENGTH: 4 metres (13 feet)

WEIGHT: 270 kilograms (595 pounds)

TYPE OF EATER: herbivore

PHYSICAL FEATURES: neck, back and tail covered with horns and plates

SCELIDOSAURUS was one of the first armoured dinosaurs.

Paleontologists once thought **SCELIDOSAURUS** ate fish instead of plants.

Scelidosaurus lived in what is now England.

N
W ← → E
S

where this dinosaur lived

SCELIDOSAURUS fossils were some of the first to be discovered.

SCUTELLOSAURUS

PRONOUNCED: skoo-TELL-o-SAWR-us

NAME MEANING: lizard with little shields

TIME PERIOD LIVED: Early Jurassic Period, about 195 million years ago

LENGTH: 1.2 metres (3.9 feet)

WEIGHT: 10 kilograms (22 pounds)

TYPE OF EATER: herbivore

PHYSICAL FEATURES: about the size of a small dog, covered with armour

SCUTELLOSAURUS had more than 300 bony studs in its neck, back, sides and tail.

Scutellosaurus lived in what is now Arizona, USA.

Two partial **SCUTELLOSAURUS** skeletons have been found.

N
W   E
S

where this
dinosaur lived

SCUTELLOSAURUS
walked on two legs.

STRUTHIOSAURUS

PRONOUNCED: STROO-thee-o-SAWR-us

NAME MEANING: ostrich lizard

TIME PERIOD LIVED: Late Cretaceous Period, about 65 million years ago

LENGTH: 3 metres (9 feet)

WEIGHT: 272 kilograms (600 pounds)

TYPE OF EATER: herbivore

PHYSICAL FEATURES: not much larger than a sheep, covered with armour and spikes

Paleontologists once thought **STRUTHIOSAURUS** was a carnivore.

Struthiosaurus lived in different parts of Europe, in today's Austria, Romania and France.

■ where this dinosaur lived

N
W ✦ E
S

STRUTHIOSAURUS and Struthiomimus have similar names. But these dinosaurs were very different. Struthiomimus had a birdlike beak and walked on two legs.

STRUTHIOSAURUS was the smallest ankylosaur.

GLOSSARY

ARMOUR bones, scales and skin that some animals have on their bodies for protection

BEAK hard, pointed part of an animal's mouth

CARNIVORE animal that eats only meat

CLUB heavy object often used as a weapon

CRETACEOUS PERIOD third period of the Mesozoic Era; the Cretaceous Period was from 145 to 65 million years ago

FOSSIL remains of an animal or plant from millions of years ago that have turned to rock

HERBIVORE animal that eats only plants

HERD group of the same kind of animal that lives and travels together

JURASSIC PERIOD second period of the Mesozoic Era; the Jurassic Period was from 200 to 145 million years ago

MODEL something that is made to look like a person, animal or object

PALEONTOLOGIST scientist who studies fossils

PLATE flat, bony growth

PREDATOR animal that hunts other animals for food

PRONOUNCE say a word in a certain way

SHIELD object that gives protection from harm

SPECIES group of plants or animals that share common characteristics

SPIKE sharp, pointy object; many dinosaurs used bony spikes to defend themselves

COMPREHENSION QUESTIONS

1. Turn to page 8. In your own words, describe what is happening in the picture.

2. What dinosaur was faster than any other dinosaur in this group? Use the text to help you with your answer.

3. At first paleontologists thought Struthiosaurus was a carnivore. What does "carnivore" mean?

READ MORE

Ankylosaurus and other Armoured and Plated Herbivores (Dinosaurs!), David West (Franklin Watts, 2013)

Dinosaurs in Our Street, David West (Franklin Watts, 2015)

A Weekend with Dinosaurs (Fantasy Field Trips), Claire Throp (Raintree, 2014)

WEBSITES

www.bbc.co.uk/cbeebies/shows/andys-dinosaur-adventures

Go on a dinosaur adventure with Andy and Hatty! Play games, sing songs and watch clips all about dinosaurs.

www.show.me.uk/section/dinosaurs

This website has loads of fun things to do and see, including a dinosaur mask you can download and print, videos, games and Top Ten lists.

INDEX